OTA BENGA

Elvis Alves

ISBN 978-0-9884324-2-0

Book Design by Tishon Woolcock
Cover Art by Chen Dongfan

CONTENTS

Ota Benga. Bronx Zoo [United States], photograph, 1910. © Coll. Part. / DR

DID YOU EXCHANGE A WALK ON PART IN THE WAR FOR A LEAD ROLE IN A CAGE?

— WISH YOU WERE HERE, PINK FLOYD

PERFECT DATE

You ask me about my
perfect date.
How it would look?
I say that it would take
place in a country other
than our own;
a city to be exact.
Preferably at the setting of
the sun.
I picture us holding hands,
strolling along the emptying
marketplace
of Paris or Abidjan.

OTA BENGA: THERAPY

America had become a cage to him,
and he longed to be free once more.

–Frederick Drimmer on Ota Benga

African man trapped in a cage and put
on display at the Bronx Zoo. Tell me what
you see?

I see them but they do not see me. Otherwise,
I would not be in captivity.

You are witnessing the presence of ignorance;
the demise of civility.

Indeed, I am witness to these and it is
killing me. Plus there is insanity. I want to be free.

African man trapped in a cage and put on display
at the Bronx Zoo, you speak so lucidly. Tell me
more about the gaze and what it is that you see?

I see humanity staring back at me. And calamity in
the wake of rapid destructive entities: capitalism,
war, and poverty.

Where is the escape, there must be a way out
of this misery? African man trapped in a cage,
answer me.

Put a man in a hole that he did not dig
and he is bound to explode violently.

You sound angry; Tell me how
you feel?

I see that you are the therapist extraordinaire.
Do you want to psychoanalyze me? Well, write
that I am from a land far from here. Survival is a must,
at any cost it is necessary. Kings rule with iron fists
and experience great kicks in turning tricks.

Wait...Wait. You are describing a fantasy.

No...No. It is my reality. Don't think that my mind
is gone just because my life is void of tomorrows. I never had to run
from a gun until I was captured by one.

I was running from those who were after me—to enslave me.
I was running to my wife and children, trying to save them
from the fate that became me.

What is the fate you talk about?

Can't you see? I am trapped in a cage and my
humanity is no longer part of me.
Psychoanalyze me. Tell the world how I used
to be.

I will tell that you came from a land far from here.
That kings rule with iron fists and get kicks from
turning tricks. And that you never had to run from a gun
until you saw me.

CONTEMPORAY VESTIGES

The Black Panther Party died the day the militant fellas
went downtown to the Government Building to protest
but were instead offered jobs.

Capitalism has a way of drawing us in with its tentacles.
If not tentacles, then with gifted hands of a skilled carpenter who
is an expert at building cages and painting them the color of the dollar.

Most rappers have babies to feed and would do anything to accomplish this task.
They walk through the war every day, if only to get street credits, collecting
bodily scars that will never go away like the fame they hope to capture some
day.

It is not a beautiful day in the neighborhood. Everything is awry.
Mr. Rogers ran away with the Big Guy's wife. I heard they went to
Hawaii for the honeymoon. Life is not child's play.

No one really lives on Sesame St except Ernie and Bert
who sleep together. The Times reported that their house was fire bombed
yesterday.

Nobody knows the reason the arson took place but all
fingers point to Oscar the Grouch.

He was, according to the report which freely cited
various anonymous sources (due to fear of retribution), seen earlier in the day
of the incident, milling about, spewing anti-gay epithets at passers-by.

No one dared interrupt him. He is known for his bad temper.

George Jetson yells mean words at the robot who is his servant. "You fucking dumb tin can."
This behavior is expected of him because his space ship is actually a slave ship. Look closer
and you will see that it is made of the same material as that of the robot.

Everything stays the same; except the rich get richer while the poor get poorer. Today a black CEO sits on the top floor of the Government Building where the fellas were offered work decades ago.

He climbed the corporate ladder—it took him years and hard work to do so—and has the bruises to show. Edwidge Danticat once told me to "keep fighting the good fight." What is the good fight?

Yogi Bear is the overseer at a plantation disguised as a park. Am I right, Boo Boo? Why is he always hungry? Marijuana opens up the appetite. Some physicians claim it cures glaucoma, fights against the effects of cancer, and has other health benefits.

Can marijuana be the weapon of choice in the fighting of the good fight?

One night, I ran into a rapper friend at a club in Williamsburg, Brooklyn. He was performing while his daddy was working in the Government Building downtown. I got to the spot late but in time to catch him doing a rendition of Ice Cube's Today Was A Good Day. That's the song that ends with the mention of AK (...I did not have to use my AK).

PILATE

Now he knew why he loved her so.
Without leaving the ground, she could fly.

   —Toni Morrison, Song of Solomon

I

The men and women who live in the commune are ital.
They do not eat salt.

There is the shared belief that eating salt makes the body
heavy, preventing it from flying back to Africa, land of
Black gods and ever-living ancestors.

In the bottom of slave ships, black men and women of different
tribes and tongues spoke a common language of suffering
and impending rebellion to each other.

"Massa head ah go'h roll" was the common slogan amidst
cries of pain caused by pressure of chains around ankles, wrists,
and necks.

The gods do not sleep. The human will to survive is not weak.
African slaves found ways to get out of chains and not be prey
to white predators.

Their voyage was not maiden. Some refused to stay on board, jumping into
waters that will forever bear their souls.

Others arrived on shores whose inner lands were already stained by the
massacred blood of innocent Carib Indians.

Free spirits running into the wild. Free spirits running wild.
The Maroons, The Maroons "Da ah wha we are."

Episode 1: "Brudda, Brudda, leh me in." A runaway African slave begged.
No was the answer. He killed himself on the way back to the big house.

II

Drums too are in the blood where their beating competes with
that of the heart, making the latter stronger, more able to repulse
evil forces.

Runaway African slaves carried beliefs with them to the safety of
the woods as they sketched war plans on matted hair.

How many animals need sacrificing before the gods are satisfied? None.
Rebellion is not prayed for. It is a given; always within and simply needs
expressing outwardly.

No leader needs anointing. Everyday a Moses is born. Sista Harriett
waded in the waters of Jamaica before crossing over to America.

"Come leh we canga li." A Papaloi named Boukman prayed.
The machetes-ready black masses walked to the plantations
to set their fellow brothers and sisters free.

III

Episode 2 (dialogue): "Me ah look fo' Pilate."
"She deh in de 'special house.' Time ah de month."

Ithiopia continues to stretch forth her strong, black hands;
forever willing to gather her children home. Yes, Ithiopia's
hands are that of a nature motherly in essence.

For now, the Rasses, residents of the commune,
burn incense, smoke ganga, and pray to Selassie while
Pilate sits in the "special house." Her power is too powerful.

Was Marley, like Muhammad, the last prophet? Come
out, Pilate, and sit on your rightful throne. Life is too
precious to have flown out of you.

Or have you prematurely achieved the objective of not eating salt, causing your rebel soul to fly back to Africa too soon?

A black woman shall lead them. Wake, Pilate, wake for you are our Boukman in this new century.

POOR HOUSE

Father sits in the living room,
a sad look is on his face as
he stares at empty walls.

Mother is in the kitchen cooking
rice in a pot whose lid becomes
undone, spilling water
all over the stove.
She stares at but does not notice
the volcanic-like eruption.

Sister is in her room
crying as her boy child
runs wild wearing soiled diaper.
His father beats her and
the more she loves him.

Brother is away in prison,
modern day slave ship built
for people that look like him.

His sons roam the streets.
One day they too will
follow him there.

Who am I? The narrator,
the other.

ATO

Ato wears his hair in dreadlocks and calls himself Rasta.
He goes to Kwe Kwe, sings reggae songs (inserting Jesus where
mention is made of Selassie), while beating drum with fingers
of ancestral rhythm.

He was the lead singer at one of these pre-wedding parties and could
not but weep, for his love was marrying another the next day.

Ato loves often but is never loved. So instead of women,
he turns to rum and ganja for a warm touch.

LaVaughn tells the story, with a smile on her face, of the night
the boys from Scotts Campbell almost pummeled Ato to death with
their fists.

He had gone to a party and made the mistake of saying
the wrong words to one of the boys' girlfriend.

Enraged, these Sons of Ogun jumped on Ato like a pack of wolves on
a dead animal and almost killed him.

But Ato did not learn to keep his mouth shut. Weeks after the incident
in Scotts Campbell, Ato began to spread rumors about Allison,
Patrick's girlfriend. Patrick was not just the local drug dealer. He was a
crooked police officer convicted of murder but was miraculously, it seemed, set
free by the powers that be.

Pinky told me that she bore witness that day when Patrick
shot an unarmed man in the back as he fled from the eyes
of Patrick's gun. At the discharge of the bullet, the man
fell, no longer able to run. Patrick walked up to him.
Pinky heard the man's cries for mercy. Patrick fired another shot.

The same force was on display the day when with machete
in hand, Patrick caught hold of Ato by the hair and took a swipe
at Ato's head. Thanks to the gods, Ato did not fall to the same fate
as the victim of Patrick's gun. He was able to flee, leaving strands of
hair behind.

Karma caught up to Patrick. The picture of his bullet soaked car and
body turned up on the front page of the Stabroek Newspaper.
A gunman killed him in Georgetown. With his last breath, did Patrick
beg for mercy like the unarmed man he killed or did he attempt to flee
like Ato?

BORICUA

She said that she has a man
but we sit and eat lunch at work
everyday. And each day, before departing
the table, she turns and asks with a coy smile
"Are you going to be here tomorrow?"

She has yet to learn my schedule
but I know hers from the first time
she told me what it was,
and so I say "Yes. I'll be here."

She picks up her tray
and walks the direction of
the dumpster.

My eyes follow the maneuvers
and curves of her backside.
They seem to call a name not
my own.

She wears a tattoo on the right side of
the neck whose letterings read Boricua.
Her father is Puerto Rican,
her mother African American.

One day she read me
a poem and even though it
was not about me I said that it was
sweet.

I CHANT

I and I chant Rastafari
speaking truth to power
while Babylon keeps burning

with holy fire.
I and I chant Rastafari
pleading Ithiopia to stretch

forth her black hands and gather
her sons and daughters from the
four corners of the world.

Bring them back to Africa, the land
of black gods and ancestors who
never really die but remain steadfast

like the pulse that beats in I and I heart.
I and I chant Rastafari so that the sleeping
bones of I brothers and sisters can wake

and walk again. I chant down prisons,
banks, schools, churches, and other organizations
that seek to capitalize and colonize I people.

I chant down facebook, gmail, twitter,
different names—same game of conquer and
claim—for the Nina, Pinta, and Santa Maria.

What a shame!
Bringing total destruction in their wake;
telling I people they cannot communicate,

live, without being bound to the invisible
chains of the Internet. I and I chant until
I can't chant anymore—which will never

happen because I and I chant endures.

FRUSTRATION ON BOARD

I entertain myself by beating
my left big toe with the reed of
the hibiscus flower plant until it
becomes purple like the teeth of the
old man who forgot what it was he
chewed just seconds ago.

I laugh twice and then cry two
more days because sorrow seems
forever on my path especially when it
rains ashen candlesticks from a sky one
inch above my head.

There is no touching like two virgins
married and one suddenly dies before
the consummation of the bond,

too much excitement for him.

And the victim must be a he because
only a man gets excited about sex.

It is a chore for a woman
and sometimes she does not want
to take part in it because there are
too many other chores in her life.

So I continue to beat my left big
toe purple and I am excited.

LUCY

FOR JAMAICA KINCAID

Lucy is not a monkey, or
any other animal to

domesticate—make one's own.
She is a black pearl. Mother to

the world. Never someone's girl.
She is an artist in the making and

hangs out with the downtown
Bohemian crowd, knowing that they

too participate in her oppression.

Her island home calls her name oceans
away. But Lucy does not listen because it

is infested with coconuts and rum. Plus
New York is where dreams come true.

So Lucy stands to fall again and falls
to stand again.

OTA BENGA: ANNIVERSARY

Live Free or Die
  --New Hampshire State Motto

There was no centennial celebration in 2006 to commemorate
the date when Ota Benga first touched the grounds of the
Bronx Zoo.

Neither is there a grave site to indicate the spot where
his 32 year old body was buried after a fatal self-inflicted gunshot
wound to the heart in Lynchburg, Virginia, in 1916.

His life's story has been wiped out from the pages of history books. He is hidden
from the collective memory of American History.

Ota Benga is gone for good. He has flown beyond the wind. In life
and death he speaks his native Tshiluba to an audience of none. They came
to see him as a spectacle, a non-sentient being, not to hear his pleas for life, liberty,
and happiness.

In his native land, Ota Benga was a husband, father, and gifted hunter. He
was brought to America to be a slave on display, and was treated as a caged
animal. In commemoration of your life, dear Ota Benga, these words
ring true: I'd rather be a free man in my grave than living as a puppet or a slave.
Peace be upon you.

YES LORD!

THE STORY OF A MAN WHOSE WEDDING
WAS ATTENDED BY JESUS

It was the wedding day of Bill Brody and Amanda Francois. The ceremony was outdoors. Amanda did not want to get married in a church. She wanted to elope to Las Vegas. Bill disagreed because he wanted his family and friends to share the event with him. A compromise was reached. No eloping. No church. The wedding was in the Hamptons where the Brody's had a vacation home.

I met Bill in college. We were roommates our first year and decided to stay so for the next three years. We were the only black guys in the dorm and felt that it was no accident that we were paired as roommates. When I married my college sweetheart, Michelle, I did not hesitate in asking Bill to be the best man. I always knew that he would ask me to be his best man at his wedding should the day come.

I was surprised—and not surprised— when he disclosed to me an hour before the wedding that he was having serious jitters about marrying Amanda.
"I still can't get it out of my head," he said.
He was referring to the time that he came home early from work and found Amanda in bed with her friend Amina. I had called him a fool for staying her with.
"I thought you were over Amanda sleeping with Amina. After all you were the one who encouraged her to get marry," I said.
"I know. But what if I am not really over it?" Bill asked.
"It's too late. Too much money was spent on this event. There's no turning away now," I retorted.

I was there when Bill told his parents about marrying Amanda. We were at brunch at a French restaurant on Myrtle Ave. I was fascinated by the paintings of black musicians and instruments that plastered the walls of the restaurant. This was one of my favorite places to eat. I've visited it several times, sometimes with my wife and other times with women that I see on the side. I always stare at the walls, trying but unable to recognize all the musicians. Other than the vivid colors, my eyes often glue to the lips of the musicians. They were big and succulent. I always joked with my dates that I bet the guys on the wall were good at pleasing a woman. In return, my dates would giggle in such a way to indicate that they agree with what I had said.

I was looking at lips as Amanda sat across from me, next to Bill, staring at her left finger. The finger was the new home of a diamond ring that would make the average woman jealous. I remember chiding Bill for purchasing such an expensive ring after he showed it to me and Michelle when he visited us a week earlier at our home in Princeton. "That is so beautiful," Michelle said, with a tinge of envy. "You made a Hasidic guy in the Diamond District very happy!" I blurted out. We laughed. After Michelle retired upstairs, Bill and I continued the conversation over cold bottles of beer while watching the Knicks on T.V. When Bill was ready to leave, I walked him to the door, gave him a hug and said, "Congratulations…just be careful." He nodded in agreement.

"This is such a nice restaurant!" Mrs. Brody's words jolted me to the fact that we were sitting in the French restaurant.
"Yes" Amanda said, taking her eyes off the ring.
"So, mom and pop, as I told you over the phone, Amanda and I plan to marry this coming summer," Bill said, looking directly in the eyes of his parents.
"Son, we are so proud of you—both of you" said Mr. Brody. It was not too difficult to be proud of Bill. He always did the right thing. After college, he enrolled in Harvard's MBA program. He makes big bucks as a financial advisor on Wall Street. Yet, he was unhappy.

He said so to me the night of his bachelor's party in Atlantic City. The two black strippers me and a small group of friends hired to perform had just finished their first set of theatrics and Bill and I stepped outside on the balcony of the hotel room for a smoke. The room was over-looking the ocean. The August night was sticky and calm. Pointing to the room and its drunk occupants, Bill said "Prostitution should be illegal."

"Stripping is not prostituting. I wish people would pay me to take my clothes off. I'll quit my day job for sure," I said. We both laughed. "Seriously, though, I've been thinking of quitting Wall Street and going back to school" Bill Said.

"What would you study?" I asked

"I'll go to seminary and become a minister" Bill said.

"This conversation is over. You know that religion leaves a bad taste in my mouth. Plus, now is not a good time to talk about these things. For Christ's sake, it's your bachelor's party!" I said.

Bill did not bring up the topic about going to seminary again until six months after the wedding.

Religion had always been important to Bill. He attended the campus chapel services every Sunday while we were in college. If I was not too hung over or had little work to do, I would go with him. The chaplain noticed Bill's affinity for religious matters and tried to persuade him to attend seminary after college. Bill did not listen then and opted to enroll in the MBA program at Harvard. This decision did not please two people: the chaplain and Bill's mother.

Mrs. Brody bleeds Jesus. This fact was on display at the wedding's reception when the mic was handed her to say well wishes to the newly married couple. I do not remember all that was said because I was already wasted by then and, in all honesty, I did not care to pay attention to that kind of stuff. I do remember hearing:

...Bill was my first child. I wanted more children but this dream became impossible when the doctors found a cancerous tumor in my womb months after I gave birth to Bill. I had an emergency hysterectomy.... This experience made me realize that Bill was a blessed child....

Mrs. Brody's speech had a long-lasting effect on Bill. He declared this fact to me six months later as we sat drinking coffee at a café on Nassau Street in Princeton. He and Amanda had filed for divorce. It turned out that Amanda's episode with Amina was not just an episode. She declared herself a full-fledged lesbian and was living with Amina in Brooklyn, in the apartment she once shared with Bill. Bill enrolled at Princeton Theological Seminary.

"So, tell me how news of your mother's hysterectomy persuaded you to quit your job on Wall Street?" I asked.

"My mother's speech at the wedding was beautiful. It drove home to me that I was chosen to do great work---God's work. I have always believed that it was not accidental that I was born before my mother was diagnosed with cancer and had to have her womb removed. I've always felt called to ministry and Jesus was at my wedding!"

I sat there listening to my friend, feeling sorry for him but knowing that things would eventually work out for him. With or without Jesus, Bill will be just fine—more than fine.

ABOUT THE AUTHOR

Elvis Alves is the author of the poetry collection *Bitter Melon*. He was born in Guyana, South America, and raised in Brooklyn, NY. Elvis is a graduate of Colgate University and Princeton Theological Seminary. He lives and teaches in Newtown, PA.